# Headframe:

BEING A Flin Flon Book with crowbars, a novel, a navel, a raven, hammers and shovels, two fish stories (in divers forms), three jokes, a puck, rink rats, four players playing, and Featuring a carnival (thanks to Andrea, Shannon, Denis, Mark and Lorraine) with guest appearances by promoters, prospectors, trappers, and suckers, as well as sundry rogues and rascals, and concluding WITH TAILINGS (which contain still m/ore to be mined), etc.

# HEADFRAME:

BIRK SPROXTON

TURNSTONE PRESS: 1985

Published with the assistance of the Manitoba Arts Council and the Canada Council. Reprinted with the additional assistance of The Alberta Foundation for the Literary Arts.

Turnstone Press
607-99 King Street
Winnipeg, Manitoba
Canada

This book was typeset by B/W Type Service Ltd. and printed by Hignell Printing Ltd. for Turnstone Press.

Printed and bound in Canada.

Cover Design: Darlene Toews

First printing, 1985
Second printing, 1986

Canadian Cataloguing in Publication Data

Sproxton, Birk.
Headframe:

Poems.
ISBN 0-88801-099-0

I. Title.
PS8587.P76H4 1985 C811'.54 C85-091381-0

*for*
*my mother and father*

Acknowledgements

Thanks for various kinds of support and encouragement to Irm Matthes, David Arnason, Dennis Cooley, Robert Kroetsch, Diane Cooley, Dave Carr, Carol Dahlstrom, Pat Sanders, Ken Hughes, and to Aydon Charlton, Angela Jeske, Gordon Turner and Gerry Brydon.

Others who helped are in the text.

Thanks also to the Film and Literary Arts Branch of Alberta Culture for a grant to assist in writing this book.

Parts of this book have been broadcast, in slightly different form, on *CBC Alberta Anthology*, and have appeared, or will appear in *CV/II, Grain, Prairie Fire, Capilano Review, Camrose Review.*

Now a Silenus, in ancient days, was a little box, of the kind we see to-day in apothecaries' shops, painted on the outside with such gay, comical figures as harpies, satyrs, bridled geese, horned hares, saddled ducks, flying goats, pot-bellied pelicans, dewy-eyed moose, bears sitting on toilets, dogs wearing socks, stags and other parties in harness, and other devices of that sort, light-heartedly invented for the purpose of mirth, as was Silenus himself, the master of good old Bacchus. But inside these boxes were kept rare drugs, such as balm, ambergris, cardamum, musk, civet, mineral essences, and other precious things.

Adapted from Rabelais, *Gargantua and Pantagurel* (1532)

Hundreds of tiny fragments of action, some leading somewhere, most going nowhere. Only one thing is clear. A fragmented game must be played in fragments.

Ken Dryden, *The Game* (1983)

stand on a horse of country
rock and look over an ore
body which is visible and
proved

Charles Bramble,
*The Land of the Lobstick* (1920)

# The Open Pit

## Night Thoughts on the Home Place

*What are you doing in there?* shouts my father
banging on the bathroom door. *Homesteading?*
And I know it is time to finish off, button up,
and get out. Time to find a place to be in,
a place
          to begin:
                              mmmmmmmmm

                                    aaaaaaaaaa

                         mmmmmmmmmmm

                                          aaaaaaaaaaaa

deep     below the surface
straining the earth
gi

gantic
magma     splits
*buckle & crack*
into basic and acidic
her contortions
wrinkle the crust
and on the seventh
granitic magmas rise


she sees it is     good
and takes her rest
magmas (now)
begin to crystallize


*(yr eyes*
*yr eyes)*

*Tumescence:* n. the swelling and uparching of a volcano during periods of rising magma preceding an eruption.

tumescence precedes essence
(tomb essence)

*Take big steps* my father says
(a footnote from underground)

*Take big steps Your shoes will last longer*

dark
out of the dark
out of the dark ground

out of the dark ground clutching
(yes) hugging their lunch pails they
come      out of a dark ground
dark      out of
the ground

## Notes from the Surface

: Underground is different from the Surface
(a fancy name for the Bull Gang, Timber Crew,
and Track Gang)

: Surface workers wear blue hardhats
(Early Wakeham has an orange one)

A guy really has to watch out for him. One day we were changing ties and he swung his pick and hit the rail. Nearly two feet of tie sticking out and he hits the goddamn rail. Sent the tip of his pick flying past my ear.

: I work on the Surface (Track Gang)

Old Dave, you know, likes having us on his crew even if he pretends to be tough. The day I had a cold and we were changing rails in the slag tunnel, he sent me down to shovel sand at forty-four fill. I needed to get away from the tunnel and he knew it.

: The Track Gang has two crews:
a Flux Pit crew and the Open Pit crew

Those new bosses from South Africa like to have everything tidy. They were flying over the plant in a helicopter and noticed old ties strewn along the right-of-way out to the flux pit. We had to go out there with the flux pit crew and pile the ties for burning. For the rest of the summer, whenever it was wet, the flux gang had to burn those old ties. They burned so many piles Blackie called them the hemorrhoid crew.

: I work in the Open Pit      clinktag thru
timekeeper's door

The most fun we ever had was the time we unloaded rails in the thaw shed. Don and I got on opposite ends and pried them off with bars. We started working as fast as we could, watching each other, timing it right, flipping the rails quick. The noise got better and better as we dumped more rails on the ground. They clattered and echoed like giant tuning forks. Old Dave was mad as hell, waving his arms and jumping around, but we couldn't hear what he said.

sleep

out of a sleep

out of your earthsleep

out of your deepsleep

out of your sleepsweet

: The Schmidt twins     doppelgangers
work in the Flux Pit

I trained myself to fall asleep at lunch time, and got pretty good at it after a while. I can sleep on rock or on ties, just about anywhere. I pull my hardhat down over my eyes and sleep until the 12:30 whistle.

The other day when I was sleeping Blackie filled my lunch pail with dandelions. He didn't let on he had done it, but I could tell by the way he laughed and carried on when I opened my pail for afternoon coffee. I kept the dandelions in my lunch pail and after work when Blackie was in the shower, I wrung those dandelions out—there must have been three or four handfuls—squeezed every drop into his snoose box. I was putting the lid back on when he came out of the shower. He stood there with a towel around his middle, looking at me and my fistful of limp dandelions, but he didn't say anything. Later I felt bad about doing that. Some guys will kid around on the job, but when you get street clothes on, they just go quiet.

: The Schmidt twins say you can hear the whistle at the Flux Pit: "Honks like a constipated goose"

## Still

an old photograph shows a baseball game
    shortstop leans back (hard grounder?)
    runner on first tilts forward
    *two down I've got to go*
    pitcher shrugs his throwing arm
        he knows his infield

    batter cursing *damn* drops his bat
        hangs      in mid-air
        just over home plate (lefty
    he has a step towards first bag)

    *Catch it this time Butterfingers*

    smeltersmoke hangs heavy overhead

someone has printed across the photo
    "World's Only Baseball Diamond
        On a Lake Bottom"

## Three Stories

"You can stand," Charles Bramble tells us, "you can stand on a 'horse' of country rock and look over an ore body which is visible and proved for 3000 feet in length by 500 feet in breadth. Flin Flon Lake is but 12 feet deep, and as there is a fall of 28 feet at the foot of the lake it will be an easy matter to run it dry."

In an interview, Gordon Brownridge says, "Anywhere from three to ten feet of muck would be loaded into cars but it was so sticky the cars had to be chained to the tracks otherwise they'd go off with the load as well. I finished pumping out one section on a barge, and down in the bottom of the lake were all the shovels, pick-axes and bars. Guys would get disgusted and just heave them."

in the

sweet

dark

earth

deep

ground dream

## The Wedding Guests

Early Wakeham jams his hooked nipping bar under the tie and leans back on the shaft, snugging the tie up to the rail. Don and I start our spikes and Early tilts his head to one side looking at weeds in the ditch and goes off into a private movie, grin wrinkling the corners of his mouth. *Whang,* Don drives the last spike home, and we scuff to the next tie.

Early stays leaning on his bar. Don and I light a smoke as Old Dave, the foreman, comes up to us hands in his pockets.
*You gonna stand there like a prick at a wedding?*
Early just smiles.

in the<br>
   sweet<br>
       dark<br>
            earth<br>
   deep<br>
ground     dreaming<br>
how<br>
  it all<br>
    depends<br>
          upon<br>
  a red head frame<br>
fingerroot         in the sweet dark<br>
                deep

## Forty-Four Fill

The story goes easy:     forty-four fill
is forty-four hundred deep feet
the hard part is to
find the right step
  : a drivestride two ties down the track
  : a mincing single-tie pirouette step
  : a tippoint toestride so light you cross yr legs
    rub yr balls & ride down the rail
    slide on its tiltshine to
chainlink fence topped with barbed wire
  of war memory & shadowlurking nazis
  with teethgleam & bombplot or dark jap eyeshine
    there on streetrock tombstone slide
    for winter boys in frostnip nights
    childsplay

(Now) sun beats the fence into day
you take a long-handled spade & go
out to the power pole
                    (mosquitomiles north at Island Falls
                     another fall we call a fall
                  charging Churchill River spins slick powerplant)
            you grasp workgear
buckle the strap round belly snug
heave hips tight to the hemp's smooth tug
   bellycord stretches & dynamo child pushes
   softsand wary to the earth's dark hole
     (narrowdeep canal crusted with fine fluxsand)
& dynamo child shuffles crosstrack
   heaves shovelhandle rightdown leftup
   throws seed for shaftfill
     fearshiver tingles thru shoulderarmknees
   shrivelled groin knows     plants feet
     hourglass sand fallingsand down
       spreads canal air 1000 2000 3000 &
delicious earthbreath bursts
    dustnoise blasts sundried surfacesand &

sweet    dark    ground

earth    deep    dream

deep    sweet    dark    earth    dream    ground

deep    sweet    dark    earth

dreamground

dream        ground

## Slag Pour July/1966

1.

After the food and stories, we left the house empty
and drove to watch the slag pour. We went through Creighton
up the twisting hill and past the place where my parents
had first loved when they came here thirty years ago.

*More a shack than a house* Mother said
*We lined the walls with old newspapers to*
*stop up the drafts*

Tells how she put bedlegs through bottoms of inverted
jam tins to keep mice out of children's beds.
The house, too, is long gone.

## 2.

sun stretches
the sky north of 54 July
is no darkness only a lesser
light
across the lake a slag train
groaning growing drowns out
the buzz of mosquitoes tracking my head
train cranks along the edge of the dump
and power poles lurch to attention in bold
red then fade to a glowing gold

train slows jerk bounce backward
topples black crust *whiteorangered*
sparksplashes down the embankment
float molten down&down the hill
footlights to the looming train: two streams
burst fire luminous fingering down

train struts to centre stage backs one
step glides to a chorus of steel on steel
one step back and disappears
without a bow
sulphur string drifts
across the dimming
lake

into the ground

into the dream

deep sleep dream

# Bitches Like Toe-Jam

## Cross the Bridge

and on, past the highway sign *Manitoba 10 South Kelsey Trail* down the hill on the bridge's south side, town side, around the corner, past the hospital *St. Anthony's* (cross perched on peak of facade) and past the alley where Noah was found, past the Cambrian Hotel where I had seen him five/six? years earlier.

—Hey Kid, c'mon for a beer. You look thirsty. Hey, Roadcutter's driving taxi in town. C'mon for a beer with us.

I was surprised by Noah's speech. In the bush he hardly talked at all, though every two weeks he wrote to his mother here in The Pas. *le pas: the stepping place* ("the first arrivals being French Canadian they called the place Le Pas—the step or strait—because of the short crossing which gave easy access to the opposite shore"). Writing was a ritual for Noah. He would take his yellow pencil stub and scrunch himself up on his cot. He would mumble and sweat, put the stub in his mouth, and mumble and gum at the same time.

I wondered what he would write about. We worked seven days a week, ten hours a day, and up to twenty hours when day and night shifts got together to move the drill to a new site. Once a week, if we weren't socked in by rain, a plane brought supplies and mail. On off-hours we slept, or played cards, or just lazed around and listened to Jean-Paul say *roger roger* on the radio phone. The only time that anything exciting happened was when a scrawny female dog came out of the bush.

## The Fabulous Story of Man and Beast at Dud Lake Camp 56/Midwest Diamond Drilling

The characters are:

DOG: she had nearly starved to death. She must have been abandoned by a trapper, and had not learned to fend for herself. She was so hungry she ate too much and got sick. Slowly she grew fat from hanging around eating our scraps. She became fast friends with

JEAN-PAUL: geologist, as silent as Noah, unless you got him talking about lichens, shot at bears in the dark, despite growls in camp from

ARNOLD: runner, younger than Jean-Paul, Ukrainian farmer from around Kamsack *What kind of a dumb bugger goes around shooting in the dark?* lean and wiry but smaller than me, the

KID: driller's helper, student, too young to work for Hudson Bay Mining & Smelting in Flin Flon, says to the men (when they ask) that *it's good experience to work* (my father's words); the men laugh Haw Haw "Work is good experience?" haw haw; learning how to work in the bush from

NOAH: driller's helper on the other shift when he's not teaching me how to (1) sharpen an axe *Run the file away from the blade, Kid* and (2) build a dock from a boat *The damned dock is too short* says Sweeny *you guys need to build onto that bugger so I can float right in. I'm not busting a pontoon to feed your fat bellies* (winking at Noah)

We build the dock, hammering posts into the bottom muck, me holding the post and hoping that Noah's aim is good. Boat swims a slow circle around the post as Noah puffs and whales away with the blunt end of an axe, and the pole jumps, sometimes sideways, sometimes upwards. It begins to sink at last and grow more steady as Noah, sweating and mumbling *Jesus it's hot Kid* takes on a greenish look belching last week's wine *It's hot by*

GEORGE: foreman, saves us from the dock building to help him find ⅝ inch nuts to repair the cat; greying a little, small and quick, always a cigarette in his mouth *rollies*; likes teasing Noah too *Noah* he says *that mouth of yours would make a curly-headed christer stand up. Why don't you grow some fuzz on it and go into business?*

Business in camp is eating and our boss is

COOK: whose name is also Cook, can make everybody miserable by cutting us off canned fruit juices *six cans each every day is too much* or by making rotten coffee or by lacing our food with so much saltpeter that no one will ever get it up again *More saltpeter than peanut butter in them cookies* mumbled Noah shaking his head.

He shook his head again when

ROADCUTTER: from Swan River, younger than me (Kid) asked how we were going to get the tripod up *Sky hooks* Arnold said *Sky hooks*. Roadcutter stayed green even after he got Jean-Paul lost in the bush.

—Hey, did you read that new novel?
—What novel?
—*Antlers in the Treetops* by WhoGoosed the Moose.
—Ahhhhhhhhh.
—Did you hear about the sequel?
—Oh no, shut him up.
—*Blazes in the Treetops* by WhoGoosed the Roadcutter.

When they found their way back to camp, drenched, no one said much. Dog skittered sheepishly under the cookshack, and Roadcutter just grinned his green grin. Jean-Paul stayed in his tent that night and cleaned his rifle.

The next morning *(Act One, Scene 1)* was sunny.

Exterior. Six tent shacks framed by spruce bush on the edge of Dud Lake. The ground slopes down toward the lake where a dock sticks about thirty feet out into the water. Two posts sit alone, twelve feet beyond the end of the dock.

*Scene 2.* Exterior. Medium shot shows a mongrel dog with some husky in the shape of her ears and tail slinking around the corner of a shack.

Close-up shows her grabbing from a small stump a grey woolen sock with a red stripe across the top. She tosses it and begins a game of tag. But the sock is too tired and won't chase her. She nips at its heel. The sock does not respond. Annoyed, she takes the sock under the tent shack to give it a piece of her mind.

*Scene 3.* Medium shot. As Dog's tail disappears under the shack Arnold comes out, yawning and stretching, and walks barefooted over to the stump where he left his socks to dry.

Close-up shows him puzzled until he spots Dog running out from under with the still sleepy sock in her mouth. Arnold starts after her, doing a crazy two-step as roots and stones stab at his feet.

*Scene 4.* Interior. Cookshack. Close-up shows Kid's hand resting on the table beside a white coffee mug. A black stripe circles its rim. George's hand reaches to take Kid's wrist and turns it to show a bruise at the base of the thumb.

GEORGE: That looks pretty bad. Maybe you'd better go to town. Maybe you need a doctor.

KID: Yeah, maybe I'll die too.

GEORGE (drops Kid's wrist and cuffs his shoulder): You know in town you could wash that in some nice crotch-juice.

NOAH'S VOICE: I know some nice girls in The Pas, Kid. They'll look after you.

*Act 2.* Interior. The night of the sunny day. Overhead shot shows hands of men in a circle of light playing yahtzee on a wooden table. An ashtray, formerly a sardine tin, sits just off centre. It is visited often by the veined and hairy-knuckled hand of George fingering a wrinkled and smoking rollie. The rollie gets whacked and then snuffed and then replaced by another, butt smoking.

NOAH (his hands do not stop moving): She's getting pretty fat that Dog there. Eatin' too many good cookies.

COOK: If you buggers would eat my cookies, she wouldn't get so many.

ARNOLD (grease-stained fingernails clicking on the table): That damned scruffy mutt shouldn't even be around here. She's chewed up half my damned socks.

NOAH (his thumb chuckling quietly to itself as it teases his forefinger): Guess bitches like toe-jam.

ARNOLD (two hands caressing and shaking the tin cup that holds the dice): I'm going to wring her bloody neck.

JEAN-PAUL (his hands are clean): That Dog, if you don't like her, I'll arrange for you to leave.

Dice roll across the table.

When we left Dud Lake we flew to another camp about 150 miles east where there were more swamps and fewer trees, none of them big enough for tripod legs. Arnold wondered what Roadcutter thought about that but he didn't say a word.

Maybe that's what Noah wrote to his mother.

## The Inland Country of Good Report

Listen. Jogging into The Pas, step after step, with sweat running down your back and collecting in your crotch, you move into another time. Time collapses. In one day in 1919 Charles Bramble travelled by train, on a steamboat, in a canoe driven by what he called a "two horsepower" Indian and finally by an Evinrude outboard. (He preferred the Evinrude.)

In 1690 Henry Kelsey also travelled by canoe:

> The Inland country of Good report hath been
> By Indians but by English not yet seen
> quickly
> Therefore I on my journey did not stay
> But making all the hast I could upon our way
> Gott on the border of the stone Indian Country
> I took possession the tenth instant July
> And for my masters I speaking for them all
> This neck of land I deerings point did call

The Inland Country of Good Report. Kelsey set up a "certain cross" in token of his being there.

## Henry Kelsey Tells the First Bear Story from the Prairies by a White Man

His skin to gett I have used all the ways I can
He is mans food & he makes food of man
His hide they would not me it preserve
But said it was a god & they should starve

*In rhymed couplets yet. Imagine.*

## The Land of the Lobstick: The Log of a Canoe Journey in The Pas District of Northern Manitoba

> The voice of Charles Bramble: "Fancy anyone residing in the West and not knowing all about lobsticks! The lobstick, dear friends, is a tree which has been despoiled of its limbs excepting a few usually near the top, and which serves as a mark, a monument, or a tribute as the case may be. The Indian has always had the lobstick habit; you find evidences of it all through the North."

When he arrived in September of 1919 to begin a tour of mining properties, Bramble found his hotel just fine *all the luxuries you can expect in a city separated by eighty miles of muskeg from a main transcontinental line.* (He was there before Noah and some friends decided to play a little joke by dragging a dead bear into the hotel and propping it up on a toilet in the men's room.)

Bramble was in a hurry to get to the property at Flin Flon and out again before freeze-up. The size of the ore body *You can stand on a "horse" of country rock and look over an orebody which is visible and proved for 3,000 feet in length by 500 feet in breadth* and the prospect of more under the lake as *there is a fall of 28 feet at the foot it will be an easy matter to run it dry* made him glad *there may be many times as much ore as has been proved by diamond drill* made him glad glad glad.

Under Flin Flon Lake (long since run dry) under ground, there is now a sunless city lit by lamps of miners (*The Sunless City*, but that's another story....)

## The Shape of Time

Kelsey wanted to explore for mines, but the Hudson's Bay Company (29 May 1710) told him to wait: "As for discoveries of mines etc. it is no time to think upon them now. In times of peace something may be done...." Time to think upon mines did not come for Kelsey. No time to think.

Time (if you think of it) took the shape of

- —English guns driving the Stone Indians *Assinipoets* south and west
- —York boats and Red River carts trailing small pox and retreating buffalo
- —railways spidering north and west from Winnipeg
- —steamboats churning on the Saskatchewan (the *Nipawin* carried Bramble and his baggage to The Pas and then to Sturgeon Landing and a canoe waiting with a two horsepower Cree)
- —diamond drills cracking the pre-cambrian shield
- —roadcutters hacking blazes in the treetops
- —hoop gangs, and bush planes, and always the snarl and rattle of mosquitoes and black flies

## Another Thought

(A crew of 1250 men built the railroad north from The Pas toward Flin Flon, a distance of about 87 miles. They started in early January 1928 and reached the mine in October.

Steel was laid in the winter months on top of the muskeg. For no good reason at all, entire sections of the road beds, tracks, and engines would just sink out of sight.)

### Another Shape

Narrow bands of fragmental rocks of volcanic origin occur at many localities within the area of lavas.... These fragmental volcanics are exceptionally well-exposed from Baker's Narrows along the north arm of Athapapaskow Lake. Here, agglomerates, tuff-like and other quartzose and slaty sediments, and basic and acidic lavas are interlayered. (W. H. Collins, Canada Department of Mines, Summary Report, 1930, Part C.)

## Waiting

The mines waited / are waiting   a long time under ground<br>
under lakes   (under sentence)   Ore, waiting   *time to think*<br>
*to be mined   minding:   the ore*

*Cuprus* said the black felt letters on the grey shirts of that baseball team. Later I learned this word was not pronounced Coopers. *Schist Lake* said other letters on other shirts. My father's shirt was yellow and the blue letters said *Mine* a place I did not own and had never been to and learned about in bits and pieces.

## Two Tables in the Cambrian Beer Parlour

1: The night Noah and I went for a beer we found Arnold there with Roadcutter. They said Jean-Paul was staying in the hotel. Noah wanted to get JP to come and buy us a beer. Arnold wasn't so keen.

"Hell, he'll probably stay in his room for fear of the bears."

"Or maybe he's afraid of the roadcutters," said Noah.

"Maybe he's busy upstairs with that Dog," Arnold added.

2: She stood up and threw her beer into the face of a younger woman sitting across the table from her.

*You bitch, you're screwing my brother.*

The young woman just wiped her face and clothes and whispered through her teeth.

*What's it to you anyways?*

## Underground

(Mine must have been a dress-up name: Underground was what people said who worked there. What does it mean?)

> *Oh the rain never…*
> *and the sun…*

Dynamite. Dynamite was a thing like blasting caps for fishing (and mining) and levelling rocks in the grounds at Birchview School      tomb it says

The day my father came home, brow furrowed, an accident underground "I've seen men move bigger rocks than that"

## Resortance

A place of resortance: Henry Kelsey's description of Deerings Point in the spring. A place of resortance for the Indians on their way to trade with the English at York Factory on Hudson Bay. Today the Trappers' Festival in winter makes The Pas a place of resortance for people to celebrate the fur trade. It's a drunken bash, a rip-snorter, a tear, an orgy: some prairie people call it a barnburner. Maybe it's a celebration of the coming spring (people in the north say there are only two seasons, winter and tough sledding).

Noah was there (thinking spring). He saw the dog races *a marvellous team of black and grey huskies, their driver standing beside them, one hand on the head of his lead-dog, the other toying with a long whip* heard the moose-calling competition *beaded moccasins and brightly-coloured toques* watched the flour-packing contest *surge about him to get a look at* snowshoe races. I don't know why he was there. He should have been in the bush until break-up. Maybe he was in town getting fitted for a set of teeth.

Anyway, Noah was there. He soaked his gums with beer in the beer parlours, tongued his lips at the beauties competing for the title of Fur Queen.

Noah was there. Except for the last day. He left the beer parlour the night before with a cramp in his gut, a fist of fiery rock *Snakey beer, Noah Go home and sleep it off*

## Henry Kelsey Tells a Medicine Story

First, a man is hired to sing and dance in the tent of the sick man. "When he has sat & sung a while to his patient he that is hired will rise up stark naked making a hideous noise & having there ready a Dish of Cold water takes a mouthful of it & spurts on the sick person so following it Close with his mouth sucks at his skin & rising from him again halls drugs or something out of his mouth & so makes his fellows believe he suckt it out of the sick person, & indeed it is hard to be perceived to the contrary...."

(Now the practised observer, he chooses the rhythms of prose.)

## In the Belly of Night

When they found Noah he was scrunched up in the fetal position, a cap of white snow over his head, hands in his crotch, and in his mouth what they took to be a double tongue were his ears, folded there as if he were talking to himself.

## A Lobstick for Noah

No one danced or sang for Noah. Oh, they searched for him all right and found him (dead), and I suppose they danced from foot to foot to keep warm and no doubt muttered the usual things you say. But no one knew why he stopped to curl up and drown in the Manitoba winter night. And now there is only a certain cross and these words, this story, talking to itself.

# Finding

*By dwelling on place we hope to get back*
*through the naming to the ground.*

Robert Kroetsch

*Wednesday, 29 June*

## Red Deer to Saskatchewan

We set out at first light (the crack of dawn as they say) with lunch, binoculars, fishing gear, maps of Alberta, Saskatchewan, Manitoba. The sun hardens into day as we drive east to Saskatoon: this part of the trip is a long approach run before we unfold the maps, read the lines (shape the journey, shape the journal) and leap into a network of artery, vein, capillary, nodes—a world with choices to be made, roads to be taken or not taken.

In Saskatoon we get a hotel room. Mark and I sleep for an hour, awakened by Denis who has been out scouring the neighbourhood for a pinball arcade. He hasn't found one.

In the early evening we head for Batoche, stopping on the way to read a roadside map painted on white boards. We cross the Saskatchewan (Gabriel's crossing) and prowl the bluff high over the river. I peer down with binoculars: pelicans on a sand bar, a derelict boat swallowing water, sticking ribs into the air. (*buffalo bones the hot dust*)

Across the road, rifle pits. We walk along the path and Denis wonders out loud, "What's so great about these ditches?" He does not see the horses and men huddling, listening for silence, afraid they will hear it.

Mosquitoes attack, we swat and dodge. They win. Again. The only sure winners, they drive us to the car.

Down to the church (looking for the bullet holes) and through the grave yard, reading inscriptions, the finger tip reading *Ou* touching *Au* the numbers and names (*a local pride*)

In the dusk, a flock of nuns settles down to a picnic dinner: they wave to us.

*Thursday, 30 June*

## Pasquia Hills (where Robert Hood got all excited)

North of Hudson Bay in logging country, we pull into a roadside turnout for a piss and find ourselves on the edge of an escarpment. The height is a surprise, the hill we stand on falls away to stretching miles of wet marsh, duck and muskrat country lit by a widening sky. (Hood's excitement—he thought this the greatest height between Atlantic and Rockies.)

Somewhere near here Hood bagged his first moose. He wanted to make a drawing and put it into a book for the good of all Englishmen, but his guides wanted to cut and quarter it, feed their aching bellies. Hood persuades them to leave the carcass, he hands out liquor—they go along with him, they'll carve the beast next morning, after his sketch. That night Hood sleeps beside the moose, snuggles right up to her belly.

(Later. Reading Hood's journal.)

It was the night of April first, 1820, and Hood knew the joke was on him. He tells how they gutted the moose and buried her insides, unborn calf and all, in the snow under a spruce. Hood and his pal, the guy who lived in a leather tent, got hatchets and made plans for the night.

> It remained for us to prevent the wolves from mangling the moose, for which purpose we wrapped ourselves in blankets between its feet and placed the hatchets within our reach. The night was stormy, and apprehension kept me long awake. But finding my companion in so deep a sleep that nothing could rouse him except the actual grip of a wolf, I thought it advisable to imitate his example as much as was in my power, rather than bear the burthen of anxiety alone.

(Why influence a friend with your anxiety?)

Hood woke to a new day, refreshed, and stomped around in the snow, trying to get going.

> At daylight, we shook off the snow which was heaped upon us and endeavoured to kindle a fire; but the violence of the storm defeated all our attempts. At length, two Indians arrived, with whose assistance we succeeded, and they took possession of it to show their sense of our obligations to them.

Even in the blowing snow, Hood had a red face.

> We were ashamed of the scene before us: the entrails of the moose and its young, which had been buried at our feet, bore testimony to the *nocturnal revel of the wolves*, during which time we had slept.
>
> This was a fresh subject of derision for the Indians, whose appetites, however, would not suffer them to waste long upon us, a time so precious. They soon finished what the wolves had begun, and with as little aid from the art of cookery, eating both the young moose, and contents of the paunch, raw.

In his cabin at Cumberland House, more or less out of the snow, Hood painted that moose. Her right foreleg lifts daintily just off the ground as she munches a sprig of dead grass. She has that cow-like manner, eye rolled back to watch you, a knowing look.

## Pasquia Hills to The Pas

We wind along the Carrot River for miles, thick bush on both sides of the road. Mark won't believe the river is there; he can't see it and the map doesn't change things.

We enter the flood plain and dikes sneak slowly out of the ground, worming flat to the river. "I was reading the map the wrong way," Mark says.

The road changes from gravel to construction gumbo and then to asphalt. The plain so flat anything vertical draws the eye. Hundreds of blackbirds dip and reel behind tractor and plough. We're watching the birds when a dog attacks from the ditch. I swerve and curse, nearly lose control. A fury to match Batoche mosquitoes.

In The Pas we edge through pedestrians and traffic. We've moved dramatically from a world of timber, through waterfowl and trapping country, across farmland, and into this. Mark sees a store sign, laughs, and copies it into his notebook vertically, the way it hangs on the store front.

Mining
Blasting
Trapping
Supplies
Sporting
Goods & (in larger letters)
FURNITURE

Three hundred years of European-Indian contact on a single piece of wood: trapping (still) in the centre of things, mining and blasting noisy on the northern limits, sporting goods and loud furniture here at the southern edge, The Pas, a playful and domesticated stepping (stopping) point, Kelsey's *place of resortance.*

In our turn we step across the Saskatchewan toward the mining world, and stop for gas at the shopping centre on the north shore. It is owned by a local Indian band and their prices are better than those in town. A Shell station operated by native people trading (mainly) with Canadians of European descent. (We're driving a Toyota, Ha.)

## Alexander Henry
## Tells a Trading Story
## (The Pasquayah Village 1775)

Henry and his crew found the village at the head of a small river which falls into the "Sascatchiwaine." And the villagers were ready for a party, a hell of a smash, met Henry's bunch on the shore.

> On our arrival, the chief, named Chatique, or The Pelican, came down upon the beach, attended by thirty followers, all armed with bows and arrows, and with spears. Chatique was a man of more than six feet in height, somewhat corpulent, and of a very doubtful physiognomy. He invited us to his tent; and we observed that he was particularly anxious to bestow his hospitalities on those who were the owners of the goods.

In Chatique's tent, the meeting began without the courtesy of a shared smoke.

> Chatique presently rose up, and told us
> —that he was glad to see us arrive;
> —that the young men of the village, as well as himself, had long been in want of many things of which we were possessed in abundance;
> —that we must be well aware of his power to prevent our going further;
> —that if we passed now, he could put us all to death on our return;
> —and that under these circumstances, he expected us to be exceedingly liberal in our presents:
>
> *adding that,*
>
> to avoid misunderstanding, he would inform us of what it was he must have.

This Chatique did—in a very exact and persuasive manner—a six foot pelican with a pot belly, making trade.

I don't think that Kelsey or Chatique or Henry or Hood gave much of their energies to moving the paddle, slipping from side to side, stroke stroke stroke, *slip*, stroke stroke stroke. I think they let the paddles pull the canoe and let themselves drift into labyrinths of thought and image, their moving forward (moving into, moving thru) driven by fingers of hunger in the gut, the remembered taste of lake trout, or the echo of the smell of a woman swinging thru the nostril hairs, beating time on hammer and anvil, riding the stirrup, stirring the blood to a drum beat, *slip* stroke stroke stroke

And when they told of their travels and adventures, were the right words there, ready-made, to be bundled up for buying and selling?

(And which is the adventure: the going or the telling, the listening or the hearing? *slip, stroke, stroke*

## The Pas to Cranberry

Once again the road is familiar. We run due north; to the west lies the water route connecting Flin Flon to The Pas. On the edge of the highway a sign: STURGEON LANDING. To most people the village is nothing but this sign, yet once Sturgeon was the head of steamboat navigation north from The Pas. Toward the end of the First World War, Sturgeon was the storage ground for the fabulous copper ore from Mandy Mine on Schist Lake.

Teams of horses hauled ore from Mandy over the ice to Sturgeon where in summer it was loaded into barges and pushed by steamboat to the railhead at The Pas    *tons and tons of it*    Ore rich enough to bear shipping over the prairies    *$8,000,000 worth of ore at the surface*    to be refined and smelted at Trail, B.C.

Bramble spoke of the mine in hushed tones: "For months the Mandy and its 20 percent copper ore had fascinated my imagination, the best I had ever known, intimately, carrying only 1.25 percent; so I stepped ashore with the liveliest anticipation, feeling that the solid flesh I had lost poling up that abominable Goose Creek, and its sister in infamy, Rat Creek, had not been lost, but given in a good cause."

a photo shows the open cut    *long*

*ladder pointing to the heavens*

they call Mandy a Glory Hole    I guess

Bramble knew

what he was talking about

*Evening, 30 June*

## Cranberry Portage

Up the long sloping hill on the south side. The old radar base—still a residential school? Bob told me once how he had tried to get his students to write the stories they heard at home, even though they were not home much. He said they didn't know the stories any more, and I wonder how much their not knowing was a way of playing safe.

Things haven't changed. The long avenue running east and west (once the portage) begins or ends in Lake Athapap. Shines in the sun. North of town—it takes just this long to drive through—the terrain changes abruptly. Muskeg and rock cuts, outcroppings (does this mean rocks not yet harvested, left out in the fields, hard to get at, bog you know and all that freeze-your-ass winter weather? And how did the crops get in? Now there's a planting for you.) The road begins to slide and tilt, shiver its way through spruce bush.

We stop at Mystic Creek. Mark and Denis find a deep pool above the rapids and start to cast into the deepest part where the fat ones are hiding. I wander with the binoculars, but the sun is too low and I can't see the birds.

listen

*rock cut*

*rock huts*

*rock house*

*raucous*

a raven

## Athapap (Little Athapap)

At our cabin here near the airport at Baker's Narrows we had to clear a landing strip for Mom to park her car, knock down trees and clean out stumps. That was in 1968, the year I first read Flin's novel, the one he was born in. I remember this because that spring we moved the outhouse and Allen carved an inscription on the inside of the door: "This hole dug by" and then my name and university degrees. The English professor finally does something useful.

That spring I took out the stumps by hand, hacking away at them with a shovel and an axe, the only tools a man can trust. Allen, who likes more complicated machines, thought that only a professor would be dumb enough to clear a stump by digging and chopping at the roots. Here, get out of the way, he said, and backed his truck up to the stump. He spun his wheels, the truck jumped, its bumper landed on top of the stump. He jammed the truck into forward gear and spun his wheels. The truck snuggled down, locking even tighter on the stump. So we dug around the truck around the stump and chopped around the bottom around the truck and got the truck from around the stump and the stump from under the truck.

(And the bumper was bent and Al was mad and he carved a story on the shithouse door.)

## Big Island

North of Athapap the highway has been rebuilt and now cuts west from the Pine Root and over to Schist Lake before angling north again.

Driving down the steep hill to park, I tell how the North End is not the end of the lake, but the middle, the northernmost point you reach by car. The end is north, there, about two and a half miles and we look toward but can't see the cabin where in spring Ray's father trapped nine bears and we told bear stories and trapped mice, dead.

Across the lake to the green-white island of poplar and birch, we swam pushing a log all the up and down way, and Calvin's wristwatch said it was forty-five or was it fifty feet deep off the blue-shingle boathouse, and the girl with curves who wanted to, wanted me to, and that summerfishing day we brought a tiny duck-fluff into the boat, his mother squawking and flapping across the bay, or picking berries blue and sweet, and on the lake rolling grey to the spruce deep shore, waves on a north wind day—it all belongs.

## On the Road Again

FLIN FLON (the sign says)
Home of Bobby Clarke

and the Trout Festival

## The Festival

a carnival squeezed into three
collapsing days of summer crazytime
canoe-racing sunshine to allnight golfing
and fishfries (brainchild of some mad poet)
dancing three days in a giant piss-up    booze-up
shake-up    rocking around the clock with Elvis
*gonna rock rock rock* with Gene and Fats
twisting into moontilt midnight swimming
of bleary-eyed bellyflopping in warmwater
summerlake
a swooning swilling
carnival
swirling
whirling
*to the*
*braww*
*dayy*

*paddling*

we rocked and churned
and dipped and ploughed
lunged forward
in a zig-zag plunge
straining at every stroke
splashing a quarter mile ahead
before they stopped
laughing long enough
to start

*paddling*

*on the midnight dock*
*fountain spray fingering up*
*sprinkling my feet and crotch*
*with hands light on my waist*
*she moves toward me*
*knees thighs belly*
*arms breast cheek*
*gives a lipsoft kiss*
*and falls*
*back into the water*

*laughing*
*in the dark*
*below*

## Phantom Lake

They fought over her
and one bashed the other
over the head
                    with a longhandled spade
pushed him off the rock
down & down to the water
below
         his body was never found

But he came back    drifting
in the morning mist
hooting thru the trees
at night    owlish
and once at the height of noon
on a windless day
                         tipped
the canoe    left it floating
floating    beam to the sun

   Now    they say    he runs
      with the whitecaps
      laughs with the loon
            & deep in the winter
      rolls with the drifting
                                  snow

## *Morning, 1 July*

   a diamond drill
shining on the street    a drill

waiting for the hunch
of three-legged lover    warm
slide of core barrel    engine's
gentle hum    and the diamond speeding
seeding water    deep in the sweet dark

Tell Denis and Mark how the driller's helper runs
up the ladder to the staging (which is not here),
breaks the plug with a roll of the wrists,
throws it hard down the chute to the runner,
spins the rod and flips it to the rack
ready for the next one.    Then down
the ladder into the shack
                                        (which is not here).

We stroke the soft wood of the coreboxes.
I tell how drillers take the core
out of the barrel and lay it in the grooves,
neat half-round grooves, smooth to the touch.
Then the helper covers the core with another box,
nails it shut (a temporary coffin) and with a soft
red pencil numbers the depth it comes from.

Sometimes (I say) the core gets broken,
dropped in the water or muskeg, lost.
On a bad day you hit gravel
or grind up the rock, make gravel yourself.
Then you have gaps. *Gaps in the record*
(which is not here)
To fill the box—you've drilled, say, ten feet
but have eight feet of core—you put in a few sticks
yourself.

(Jean-Paul, reading the core:

"You guys drilling for wood?

You think a forest grows down there maybe?"

## *2 July*

Boys fishing in steady rain at Jan Lake. Too wet to search for birds. Buy a map and sip coffee. The lake is on the route from Beaver to the Churchill system. The lake full of stories, waiting for Sorestad and his poems.

## Alexander Henry Goes Fishing (Beaver Lake, November 1775)

A happy place, even before gold was found.

> We crossed Beaver Lake on the first day of November; and the very next morning it was frozen over. Happily, we were now at a place abounding with fish; and here therefore, we resolved on wintering.
>
> Messrs. Frobisher and myself were continually employed in fishing. We made holes in the ice, and took trout with the line, in twenty and thirty fathom water, using whitefish, of a pound weight, for our bait, which we sunk to the bottom or very near it.

(He found the bottom easy enough.)

> In this manner I have at times caught more than twenty large trout a-day; but, my more usual mode was that of spearing. By one means or another, fish was plenty with us; but we suffered severely from the cold, in fishing. On the twenty-fifth, the frost was so excessive that we nearly perished. Fahrenheit's thermometer was 32 below zero in the shade; the mercury contracted one-eighth, and for four days did not rise into the tube.

## Depth Sounding

: The road switches and dips, slips and dekes, almost every hill and curve is blind. The bush is thick, pushes its way onto the road.

: A cold night, ice just off the lake, no cloud cover. Overhead a slender moon carved like a trap in the sky, the snapping of stars.

: "No problem," he said. "Beds, a stove, pots and pans, everything we need is there."

: We have beds all right, but only a single mattress, and no bedding. We have a stove and pots and pans, too, but the stove has no pipes.

: Cold, ball-shrivelling cold. Gil crawls under the mattress. Tom and I make ourselves cocoons with old newspapers. We don't read them. We don't sleep either.

: We listen to the radio *voice of the north* a man's body found huddled on the beach, his canoe, an empty shell over-turned, a hundred yards away. (People say he was on his way back to the island)

: When I see Tom in Halifax, he gives me a depth map of the lake. I am pleased, love old maps, the names. Amisk, Missi Island, Comeback Bay, Denare Beach (*the filleting plant*), Sucker Creek, Sturgeon-Weir River, Crater Island, Warehouse Bay.

On the outside fold, the map says, "Allah does not count against a man the days he spends fishing."

: The map was prepared by the Saskatchewan government in 1959.

: This story is true.

## *3 July*

Al says to try Meridian Creek, what used to be called Sucker Creek. The road south from Denare Beach is what it was years ago, blind hills and curves. We get to the creek, a filleting table and boat launch on one side, a cookhouse on the other, above the rapids.

We spot a bird perched on a rock, orange breast and odd-shaped feet. Try to read identifying marks. The colours and feet are striking, the shape ungainly. I think it's a merganser. (Forgot my book.) In flight it follows the course of the creek, low to the water in a graceful sweeping curve.

I walk south toward the Sturgeon-Weir, stop at the edge of the lake. I can't see the other side. With the binoculars I bring into focus a flock of pelicans, a few small islands. This is the widest part.

Lake and river. Stories about the lake and Beaver Lake Road were my first fish stories (what was it, 128 curves in twelve miles?), and my trip here as a kid, the only time I went fishing with my father (no, we were out in a boat on Big Island once—I don't remember remembering this before). Somewhere along here I asked how wide the lake was.

The road then was new, ended at the river. It was supposed to connect with a road from the south, a short route for us to the farm. The road has not been finished. It just stops, no bridge, no road on the other side. Just the spruce-deep bush and roar of the rapids.

(Because of the rapids, the Canadiens called it La Rivière Maligne, the wicked river: the practical English renamed it the Sturgeon-Weir. River as spirit, river as producer. Two rivers. Sucker or Meridian Creek: the river as food—we're all suckers at first—river as map. Amisk: Lac aux castors: Beaver Lake. So the naming goes.)

On the edge of the road, men load a canoe onto a station wagon. Caught their limit they say, but only a few are pickerel (Jack don't count). Don't have much to say. I'm a stranger with binoculars. Maybe they think I'm a game warden. Must have taken more than their limit.

Back to the boys, the rush of the creek growing louder. They gesture to me.

Mark handles the line, gentle, easy, knowing it's alive, pulls in a pickerel flashing gold in the sun.

"We're staying," he says. "We're catching fish."

One, two, three, four pickerel, they've thrown Jacks back in and already their stories tumble one into the other and fish were plenty with us, multiplying in their way, growing bigger and more fierce, filling the seas of the earth.

A woman picnicking with her children gives me a plastic bread bag to put the fish in.

## *Evening, 4 July*

power poles anchored
in log crib loaded with rock
we grab the wire fence
pull ourselves up

North Main leans to the east
pulled down by thick shadow

the flat thaw shed
eases away from the slope
catching the sun
on squat grey walls

between headframe and shed
shadows fall upon shadow
filling the open pit

Denis turns,
"You worked down there?"
he wonders his blond head
framed by the shade
of massive black falling
upon itself
pulling

"Just around the edge," I say

holding the wire

touching the rock

shaping

the pit

# Document Section

walking
 into a library of shining woodtop tables with
crumpled-up graph paper and candy wrappers and eraser
bits and along the shelves *1913* *1914* one year per volume
*1915* each a handful *1916* numbers leading and turning

the pages, edges browning (*The Canadian Mining Journal*)

a world of print, a world of
columns & short
notes, bold headlines
*watch for the headlines*
technical articles, maps,
economic reports, a balance
of lines, mined ore body
problems, some dreadful
poems, rhymed to death

(we make our way)

The feel of the paper (glossy), the smell of yellow-dust as I turn the pages, the clarity of black & white photos, the trail of other readers (all the nickel mining items ticked with a soft lead red pencil)—these things cannot be stuck into this book, the one in your hand.

You add these touches yourself.

(I like your hands)

1.

## Wandering Men

Beaver Lake Mining District, Saskatchewan

GOLD—The first gold discoveries were made by Messrs. Mosher and Creighton in August 1913. Since that time a large part of the country around the north end of the lake has been staked. Many of these claims are of the usual *ho hum* type located during a gold rush. Even on claims where quartz veins have been found little work has been done.
—E. L. Bruce, *Canadian Mining Journal* 1 August 1914.

wind
carving
waves
lap
rock
on
shore

walking
thru the bush
    poplar spruce birch
    face-slapping willows
    wet-snow puddles      spring
    of soft muskeg

walking, looking
for gold, stooping
to scratch the rock      he finds:
a book      a small handful
a golden book      still readable
only the ending      (torn out)      gone
    nowhere to be found

he puts the book
into his pocket
without closing it

walks on, looking
for gold      he walks on
    gentle rolling country
    spring of soft muskeg
    tamarack      jackpine      willow      spruce
        birch

rocks:
fist size, skull size, thick
flesh on rock: making a shape     shaping
fire     handslap     waveslap     shaping
rock     wind:     carving waves
lap of water
snap of fire
sizzle of snow

smoke smell: fire

to smoke to sky to snow to water to rock
to
fire

somewhere else on the surface
tea boils over an open fire
and      yes      licked by tongues of flame
a rock flowers in a snap of steam
unfolds itself lovely to the gentle hand
the loving eye
                    desire finding itself

    reading
                    the rock
          reading
                    its
                        core

(i took him there
  in my canoe
                    he lost his hat

(: we sure laughed a lot)

a cone shaped mouth
   wider than a man's reach:
we panned some surface dirt
   *shake   rattle   swish*

laughed till the tears   (rolled)

   Gold   Gold   Gold

"This must be old Flin's hole."

"Ha. Dropped some on the way
      out."

crack
of
stone

sun

streaked
sky

a
leaf

snow crunch
  a path
      twisting

When they stopped on the lake to piss, Tom had the advantage. He could finish, underline it, and sometimes, on a warmer night, draw a circle, Tom in the centre. But David had trouble. Do you dot the i as you go, or pray for enough pressure to dot it after that last damned painful curving d? (Never underestimate the pleasures of a short name.)

dance in the moonlight
  glide with the drifting

snow

You know already that a mining story is a story of love, and that tiny things — the trace of perfume in the air, a tongue on a lip, a wisp of hair on the ear — mean almost as much as shouting or slam-bam fucking. Take it slow, you often say, take it slow. Loving, like mining, goes slow. There's the moment of excitement at the beginning when desire is more wish than flesh and signs are magnified by the wish. Then there's just plain delight as the wish becomes flesh. But then, too often, too soon, comes a shadow, something teasing you, not yet imagined into the world, but lingering in a web of half-told tales or lying on the tip of the tongue or the wrong end of your pen, something there, but just out of reach. And you turn your eyes in a new direction.

wandering men
tapping the face of the country
caught now in black & white
hooked
        out of time

1
  behind David's eye
  a shy wish to be soft-footed in muskeg
  and bush or facing the wind
  in a canoe    instead of here
  with children & women & family extended
    across the page    a cabin
    (syllable, says Frank, in a long
                        articulation

2
  and Tom framed
  by the doorway smiling
  other men to his left
    and in the foreground a snarl
    of curling husky    snapping
    at the camera    baring
    his teeth    thinking *meat*

3
  a hockey picture    skates & stick
  manager in long coat with fur collar
  itching for the next big game
  other men to his left    the *comitatus*
  smiling    hands in his pockets
        and in his head
                    (sentence of the future
          a buzz
              of bush planes

this site has been mined out
nothing here but country
rock

## 2.

## Look What Happens

This is the plant
that grows in the town
    (see the red headframes)
that rose in the bush
that graces the rock
that cradles the lake
that blankets the ore
that grew in her belly
    big in the sweet dark earth

*a motherlode:*

The story changes a little every time it is told. We know for sure there were two main characters and two discoveries.

One summer Tom Creighton found a novel in the bush. In the novel, our hero, nicknamed Flin Flon, dives into the centre of the earth in his man-made fish. He wants to prove the centre is inhabited. But the ending of the novel is missing, nowhere to be found. (You see how it goes: FF is the third character.)

David Collins made his discovery while boiling tea. He was on a peninsula near a strange conical formation in the rock. He was slapping his hands to keep warm. He slapped them again when he saw mineral-bearing ore peeping out of the rock, stringy little eyes winking *blink blink* at him.

David took Tom to his find, and Tom thought, so the story goes, that Flin must have escaped from the earth through this cone.

Aha, he cried, look at this, look at this, this     leaping in the brilliant sun.

## Drilling at Flin Flon Lake

The diamond drills at Flin Flon are shooting down through the ice at a small lake near the Apex claim. It is proposed to drill on the ice as long as possible before the break up, when the work of drilling will be shifted to the shore. A thorough test of the orebody will be made, and it is stated a dozen holes and more will be driven through the sulphides to reasonable depths.

*CMJ* 1 April 1916

In those days drillers had to lug gas out to the site in five gallon jerry cans. That's how you recognize an old driller—his knuckles are callused from dragging on the ground.

build your house on rock, not sand
build your house to last
build your house on rock, they said
the earth will hold it fast

Stories: a network of rumours, pretexts, lies, false leads, gaps, deceptions, love. At first, he was a hole in the ground on a narrow peninsula in a small lake, then he joined the body of stories of the north and began to shout and rant all over the bloody place *did ya hear the one did ya hear about* Once he got out of that book, there was no shutting him up.

drilling at flinflon

sudbury april 1 the diamond drills
on the great west sulphide mines at flin
flon were put in operation early last week
and the first core of the drilling *sniff*
*sniff* was brought to the pas on sunday mr
hammell brought the core in and he is greatly
enthused about it *slluuuurp* mr durkin the
drill contractor returned with him and his
enthusiasm knows no limit *whoopee yaahooooo*
says it is a remarkable sight to see an
orebody stripped *naked down to the veins*
for 200 feet and every foot showing solid
ore *hee hee* very earnestly recounted the
features as they appeared *eyes gleaming*
*a drop of sweat* and he declares *on the*
*nose* he will stake his *if you listen very*
*carefully* reputation on the favourable out-
come *you can hear him standing on the*
*horse* of the drilling *scraping one foot on*
*the heel of the other*     *staring*
*thinking*     *of a city*     *where the rain*
*never falls and the streets are paved*
*with gold*   *gold*   *gold*   *GOLD*
night and day shifts *just think* are
being worked on the diamond drills and more
men will be placed to work as they are
secured it is a rush order and minutes
are valuable to the workers *and the owners*
*too*

In The Pas District

The Pas *Herald,* April 21.—The diamond drill operations at Flin Flon appear to be satisfactory. The drillers and engineers are loath to say what the results amount to, and any reliable information is difficult to secure. The *Herald* depends upon its source of information from trappers, dog mushers, and teamsters, who worm it out of the drillers and engineers in an innocent, unsophisticated manner, and everybody is made happy about it. *Happy happy happy*

—*CMJ* 1 May 1916

The Pas was "known to the Indians as Opa: a narrow place, or Paskweos: narrows between two high places." Kelsey called this area the Inland Country of Good Report.
Flin's country.     In land.     Under lakes     under ground
...i the money

Another voice:
"That was the code in those days. If a man gave his word, well, that was it.
So David took him to his find."

*The city is called Esnesnon. This is true. The streets are paved with gold and the king wears a crown of tin tin tin tin.

And the king is a mere figurehead, a dummy you might say, and the women run everything.

And Flin got himself into trouble, as usual, and the streets are paved with gold.

Mining News from The Pas

The Pas, May 5—Messrs. Woods and Stanley Simpson got in from Flin Flon Monday noon, with diamond drill cores, after a most difficult journey by dogs and canoe. They were twice upset in crossing the ice-strewn lakes between Athapapaskow and Cumberland House. They picked up a lost traveler between Cumberland and Beaver.

The Indians called it "Athapapuskow Sakahigan" which means "rock-on-both-sides-lake" (in a bad translation). We just call it Athapap, a short name

for swimming under the trestle at limestone narrows
afterhiking from campwhitney n fishin w/al en winterton
bay      orange lichen quilting steepslant shore & hmmmmm
ssski splash at sourdough      n bakers n 3 feet v bottom glub
tip glasses grabbing glub n hhhh ch    chc hhh
cho      chuh

The names (stories) shape the map
colour it Algonkian now, now French
and always the money sings
roll with the whitecaps
laugh with the loon
dance thru the drifting
snow

## Chatique Makes a Visit
## (A Rum Story)

We had supposed the affair finished; but before we had proceeded two miles, we saw a canoe behind us. On this, we dropped astern, to give the canoes that were following us an opportunity of joining, lest, being alone, they should be insulted.

slip stroke splash

Presently, Chatique, in a solitary canoe, *rushed* into the midst of our squadron
spear in hand
demanding a keg of rum
threatening to put to
death the first that

We saw that our only alternative was
to kill this daring robber
OR
to submit to his exaction

On receiving the rum, he saluted us with the Indian cry

uuuHHHHUUUUUUUUUHHH

and departed

An Englishman uses the French (Canadien) translation of an Algonkian name to tell about a Cree chief speaking the code of the north
and rum? from the West Indies?
and Indian? Ha

We were visiting at his cabin, a fine sunny afternoon, when he asked me about it. I gave a pretty lame answer. I said that nicknames grow up because people who live and work together so closely get to know each other well. That's what I said then, but I don't really believe that. I think nicknaming is a way of telling a story or making a poem. The name Boxcar Annie tells a story—you may not know the whole story, but its shape is there, squeezed into the name. It's there Annie has a story, you could say that she lives in the story, and her story is "boxcar." We don't tell it, we just say Boxcar Annie.

Everyday we tell stories like this—making people into characters for our fictions. Barnyard Ted or Sheepshit Stan or Sidekiss—they're all stories. There may be affection in the stories—I think Boxcar Annie must have been loved—but mostly we use nicknames to keep people in character. They try to grow and change maybe, but we keep sticking them back into character. Sometimes I think we do it out of love, but sometimes I think it's a mean thing to do.

## The Pas

The Pas, May 19.—Reports from the diamond drills at Flin Flon and Schist Lake say the work is going ahead without a hitch. At Flin Flon the drills are on their eighth set, and the ore-body is considered fairly well proven up. The average vertical depth attained is put at 900 feet. That the body is lenticular is indicated at both places. The Schist Lake drill is at its third set of holes. Mr. Callinan says the ore is very heavy at Flin Flon, only taking seven and a half cubic feet to make a ton. He thinks the permanency of the deposit is well-established.

*CMJ* 1 June 1916

sun

lake bush

shield

sun & shield & lake & bush & lake & bush & rock & lake &

Flin was there before the town was.

The town lay quiet, gestating, not yet fully imagined into existence, flipping and wiggling and squirming and smiling, mostly just lying there, waiting.

Maybe a long gestation means a long life—stories which are enduring (endearing) are a long time in the making, passing from mouth to mouth, on the tip of a tongue, the verge of speech. Flin knew this and refused to stay in his novel (the one he was born in). He slipped slowly out out of the book, stepped with one foot and then the other into the context (con games) of the great Manitoba mining adventure

a few legitimate prospects and a good
many cats and Glory Holes

three principal actors: the prospector
the promoter, and the
sucker

redfaced he stepped
into a community of songs and novels
and love stories
on everyone's
lips

## Fragmental Rock

O David and Tom came to pick and to see
the rock of the crop and the crop of the rock
came just to pick and to see

a pit in the rock
a book on the ground
a town in the bush

all found    they were found ♩
by a prospector tramping around
& a trapper boiling his tea
yes, a trapper boiling his tea

O David and Tom came to pick and to see
came just to pick and to see

Flin sits on the shoulder of Douglas Durkin, just out of eye-shot, (*a dancing of rocks*) and whispers a story (*and they sing*) a past    oral romance    (*O they sing*)

> Face downward she lay in the full flood of the sunlight and gazed long at the swirling water breaking against the rocks below. A little pathway dropped from above by slow degrees to the level of the water beneath the falls and ran into the hidden corner that held the eddying pool in which she took her morning plunge.

(I wonder what she sees in all her gazing? Can she see the lens, see through the lens, down to the sunless city? Or does she find herself, a young woman in the sunlight looking down with hair falling forward and shading her eyes? What does she think about Bramble's desire to drain the lake, empty her little private pool?

In the warmth of her sun, she probably doesn't notice the water splashing from the falls onto my copy of her book, staining the pages and making a ring between the title *The Lobstick Trail* and the subtitle *A Romance of Northern Canada*. The cover is not damaged, though: the dogs still run through the bush, their master driving beside them, a lobstick in the background. Does she hear the dogs? Does she know her book is green?)

There are different ways of being bushed. One time we were drilling at the bottom of a clay ridge and pumping water from a creek on the other side about 1200 feet away. Carrying gas up that ridge to the pump wasn't hard, but the mosquitoes were mean and thick. I puffed a cigarette up that hill to keep them off my face. I didn't realize what I had done until I tripped over a root on the way back and spilled some gas on my shoe. Luckily, none of the other guys were around. They thought I was spruce happy (*running thru the bush like a bear cub with his first hard on*) but I didn't want them to think I was stupid.

something to be said about opening
a book    opening a mine:
the tip of a prospector's pick
(watch how you say that)
cleaves a line    opens a plane
in the rock face    fingers
and thumb lift leaf from leaf
and in the book we drink in the world
read the story the rock tells
mind the ore    take it all in
suckers again

this is the book
that lies in the bush
that graces the rock
that suckles the town
that rose on the lake
that waves on the shield
    where David
    where Tom

        (where you and I)

            came

# A Likely Story: The Sub Text

# THE SUNLESS CITY

WITH AN AUTHENTIC ACCOUNT

OF

*ΟΙ-ΠΙΘΗΚΟΕΙΔΕΙΣ-ΜΕΣΗΣ-ΤΗΣ-ΓΑΙΗΣ-ΟΙΚΕΤΑΙ*

BY

J.E. PRESTON MUDDOCK

AUTHOR OF

"MAID MARIAN AND ROBIN HOOD," "STORIES, WEIRD AND WONDERFUL," "FROM THE BOSOM OF THE DEEP," "THE DEAD MAN'S SECRET," "SWEET DOLL OF HADDON HALL," "STORMLIGHT," "FOR GOD AND THE CZAR," ETC., ETC.

*From the Papers and Diaries of*

*the late* JOSIAH FLINTABBATEY FLONATIN, Esq.


LONDON

F. V. WHITE & CO. LTD.

14 BEDFORD STREET, STRAND, W.C.

1905

Yes, a city deep in the earth,
a deep novel in the bowels of a deep poem,
a novel thick with plot, theme, wit, learning,
chapters, and good clean fun (three bags full).

When we read novels of an underground city, strange and wonderful things happen to us.

> Even if the image is unparticularized, the person unknown, the outlines dim, we respond immediately with fear, interest, concern, sympathy, horror, incredulity—for thoughts of death are evoked. Images of descent, of the body lowered into the ground, lying underground    *under lakes    dark as a dungeon*    frighten us with apprehensions of our mortality.
> —Blanche Gelfant, *Sewanee Review* 1975
> (she understands)

How much more evocative and exciting therefore to read about a hero like Flin Flon, his story cast in solid rock, the outlines crystal clear.

Yes, fearing death, both his and ours, we feel all prickly when Flin lies on the surface, lies underground. His colleagues got the heebie-jeebies when he talked about the lake.

The Lake of Mystery

ENTER ONE LAKE
VOICE UNDER

> For generations learned and scientific men puzzled their heads about this mysterious sheet of water, which takes all in, but apparently lets nothing out....

Flin soon caused a ruckus, a hubbub, a brouhaha (chuckling in his cups):

> "I say there are rivers and seas in the centre of the earth, and I wager (puff, strut) that the interior of the earth is inhabited."

Some say FF was driven by the loss of his lady-love, some say he was under the influence. Gravely ill, say some, gravely ill.

*Nuts*, say others.

> "I shall find a new world, a new race of beings, a land of beauty and plenty."

The co-ordinator smiled and nodded, I'll talk it over with the chairman, who nodded and smiled, and took it to the dean, who nodded ten times and smiled and talked to the president who scratched and wondered about the bottom line as

Flin Flon's Fish

Flin plunged in his man-made fish down to the bottom of the bottomless lake and landed

solidly on his head and started to talk and talk, even though there was no one to listen (but you).

The Start

> The songs of the birds were hushed, and a myriad voices of chirping insects had taken their place. Fire-flies were everywhere. They flew over the water until it seemed studded with reflected stars *twinkle twinkle* The clouds had lost their coloured light, but seemed to give off a soft silver-like radiance.

Flin woke to the echoes of his own voice as usual, and sniffed some snuff, backhanded his nose, and cast off down the river in his fish, and just huckleberried along, playing with his throttle, now slow, now fast, taking it all in, forest and jewels and all, drifting on the river cruising down the river on a sunless undernoon, drifting in his mind's eye

The Sea of Echoes -

soft fluffy clouds, bosom-like, rolling and multiplying, breast upon breast, peach-coloured nipples, furry lips pouting pink and red and vermilion, the tip of a tongue, tresses of gold and brown and auburn and black, eyes sparkling, a trace of love-must tickling the nostril

Flin Flon Has a Strange Dream

when suddenly a beach beckoned    bent forefinger
arching    Oh    ooo (hot)    ooh (warm splash)

beckon    beckon    wave    wave

and: z z z z z z z z z z z z z z a p, a flash
of lightning and a flourish of trumpets and he saw

An Electric Storm

a beach polished and worn smooth by the sweet slap of waves.

He jumped up and ran to the nearest boulder.

It weighed many tons.

It was gold.

The whole plain was gold.

The Valley of Gold

Gold was everywhere.

Imagine Flin's reaction to his find. (1) He leaned over the edge of his fish and picked up a tiny stone. (2) He lifted his chin and turned the gold in his hand, gently, as if it were fire.

The rock sprinkled crystal spears, became its own sun and as he looked into its shimmering light a wee tear formed in his eye and dropped on the stone, split and refracted the gleaming surface, and he thought of gold on earth and the sun in its heaven.

And there niggled into his mind a sharp
little niggle— a mountain of gold caught
in the
centre of earth caught beneath the
mysterious sheet.

He did the only sane thing a man could do—he took a snort of snoose, stuffed his fish full to the gills with gold, and fell in love.

Differences of Opinion

Some say his fall had nothing to do with love but was merely greed. Some say Flin was so puffed up he fell over from the weight of his arrogance. And the meeting began with a roll call and he handed me a long list of names and they are all present:

It Is Not Always Pleasant to Know What Other People Think About Us

Christer, Curly-headed
Flycatcher, Ninnie-hammer
Rascal, Mangy
Sleaze-bucket, Fat Mouth
Twaddletrap, Twittwat
Whoremonger, Shitsniffing
Wormsweat, Willywiggle

And their friends. Namecalling can be fun; I myself have a list of abusive phrases I keep for special situations but you know how it goes

The miner's notion of value, like the financier's, tends to be a purely abstract one. Does the defect arise out of the fact that every other type of primitive environment contains food, something that may be immediately translated into life — game, berries, mushrooms, maple-sap, nuts, sheep, corn, fish — while the miner's environment alone is — salt and saccharin aside — not only completely inorganic but completely inedible?

Stings, don't it?

Let us therefore contemplate some beauty to soften the blow, massage our morale.

The Beautiful Princess

ENTER BEAUTY

"Dear me, can it be possible that you are such barbarians!" cried the Princess in astonishment, as she played with a large feather fan. "The gentlemen make advances to the ladies?" she asked with a look of incredulity; and then breaking into a little laugh she added, "No, it really cannot be possible. You are given to joking, you naughty little fellow, and you are trying to deceive me." And clipped him on the ear with her fan.

Struck Flin was with her beauty but also a tiny bit annoyed at her impertinence.

On the surface of things FF thought himself to be a favourite of the softer sex. But here they fastened on his most endearing little faults and foibles, even the media got involved.

ENTER ONE MEDIUM

> In form, he is somewhat like a pre-human-being, but he is perfectly tailless, and his head is white and highly polished, and quite destitute of hair, with the exception of a little fringe round the back part of the skull. Anything like symmetry of beauty in the creature is entirely wanting. His arms are long and ungraceful, and his legs are twisted. He is small in stature, and wears over his eyes peculiar pieces of glass, which are bound in small frames that are apparently made of common gold. It would seem as if this yellow stuff had some peculiar fascination for the unfortunate barbarian, as all his pockets were filled with it.

Yes, Flin learned a hard truth, but he was an outsider, and the outsider always wins the heart of the beautiful heroine, and the logic of desire took its course and she fell in love with him. It took some doing—her parents had to insist on Flin's bad points (a long list, ugly perverted stupid said she no tail at all said he outside agitator said she no tail they said together they said)—but the lovers made out okay.

An Artful Little Puss

Come closer and I'll tell you
*whisper whisper*
(the inside story (:) a pussy poem)

a delectable ,
fl , pp, ng , ,
her tail
met the stiff :
&
made
;
(love)

But it didn't happen right away and delay heightens desire so we need an irrelevant chapter which even in a loosely organized work is a challenge and a threat

ENTER ONE PLEASANT SOCIETY

which, joined together by a need to natter, nag, moan, complain, bitch, grump, sneer, sulk, and belly-ache, started to lament the strange love (gnashing of teeth and embarrassed sniggers) between Beautiful Princess and FF, that disgusting little creature.

This Chapter Though Not Pointed Is To the Point

________ in particular, a model of rectitude, trailing gobs of platitudes, grieved that the ugly outsider was getting all the attention *sniff*, and when Flin started to preach that men should assert their independence from women, well, his message was clearly preposterous and proved conclusively the unenlightened state of the outsiders if the lack of a tail was not proof enough if you think of it *rustling of chairs*

Mr. Flonatin Gets into Trouble

ENTER ONE COMMITTEE

Red Tapeism

they nodded and smiled and talked and nodded and smiled and checked the bottom line    Touch base with me    Feedback    you know but some thought he said feedbag (three bags full) and the committee was struck and in spite of the strides of alimentation and defecation the secretary lapsed into terminal writer's block and the chairperson couldn't find the meeting room and they knew he was guilty guilty guilty guilty guilty guilty guilty

The Trial

and gave Flin a sentence without an end stop

A Journey
of Discovery

and there are worm lines to other universes, time tunnels and time machines that bring you back to where you started before you fell into a burning ring of fire and all that hard cash down down down and around the hole the flames went higher in regions where you have to travel at the speed of light in order to remain in the same place and five billion years from now the sun too will become a red giant

The rest you know already: FF talked BP into leaving with him to climb into the full light of the sun, but on their journey he looked back and (so)

fear
interest
concern
sympathy
horror
incredulity

Flin's Return
and Reception

Old Flin, much saddened and silent for once, went on alone and stepped out of the hole slowly, one foot after the other, climbed out into the day and the pocket of Tom Creighton, looking for a better ½, etc.

The Chinese tell a story of the celestial stags who live underground in mines, talking to the workers and offering to lead them to rich veins of silver and gold if only they might be released into the light of day. Miners have followed the stags only to disappear, never to be seen again. In some mines the stags outnumber the miners and cause all sorts of trouble. They roar and bellow and stamp and shake their antlers and shake the timbers and then the miners have to wall up the beasts in order to work or sleep.

# Another Belly Button

## Opening

Think of a novel found in the bush by a prospector looking for gold. He reads the book through, except for the ending which has been torn out. He is taken to an ore discovery by another prospector, and the lake near the find is given the nickname of the hero in the novel—Flin Flon. Later, the lake is drained, a mine goes down, a town grows up. The town is linked to the south by a railway and twenty years later by a highway. The town dangles there on the edge of the Laurentian shield at the end of the line, an infant, and at the mother end: a novel/navel.

This is a story of that novel mother and child.

1.

opening
a book    opening a mine

we drink in the world
read the story the rock tells
mind the ore    take it all
in

: You remember that stuff about building your house on rock instead of on sand? Well, the town is built on rock and on story. You might say it is built on (*out of*) the open pit, too.

The rock gives form
the story gives character
and the pit
makes
an opening
a place to begin

(and the ending?

*torn out*
*nowhere*
*to be found*

I want to tell
what an open pit is:      the pit open
is a hole, an absence. It has presence
    if you think about it
or if you fall into it, or stand
near the edge and think of the ground
up meat you would make falling
falling feet to the sun. But to open
the pit is to show

no lake lying over the ore-body,
a beautiful girl with long hair
peering into the water, *gone*      her
waterfall, her bathing pool    *gone*

no horses of country rock, the absence
of Bramble's horse, no cows, no moose, or
pelicans. No fat trout, no golden pickerel
shining in the sun. No man-made fish.

no Bramble

44 diamond drill holes, all driven
before July, 1918, Flin's escape hole,
gone. They just disappeared, the whole
bunch of them.

the muck gone (most of it) great gobs of
ooey gooey sticky stinky lake bottom

no stair case pitched down & down
the rock face, climbing and falling, a
hundred big steps, and more, all gone

no lens-shaped ore body 2593 feet long
bearing 16, 600, 000 tons of ore *gone*

no allusions to (1) Dante (2) the debate
between Plutonists, who favour fire as the
source of rock, and the Neptunists, who favour
water *From what I've tasted of desire*

no volcanoes rumbling rumbling heat
to the sun

built on an absence, then, a deep cut
*ab* = out, away, from *sence*

2.

something to be said about finding
a book    opening a mine
a map of references wandering & me
andering into a library becoming
solid taking on the flesh of book
signature and spine and leaf
word becoming object in the world
bending the shelf and stretching
the arms to read it
    (a refined refinding)

: Medical books say that gall stones may be related to diet but I know better. I swallowed them with the air I breathe. But I think they're gone now so I don't dream about them anymore though I still have rocks in my name (gall in my book).

burden:

the refrain or chorus
of a song, a leading
idea of discourse

something to be said

something needing
to be said

badly

well

3.

something to be said about a red
headframe    finger root deep
in the sweet dark earth
standing up    standing up
steep in the sun

: Stretching over the rocks they sprawl in a series of rises and levels and reversals—easy stages, not too steep—but I never get them to come out to a hundred. You climb them again and again and never get the satisfaction of counting to a nice even round one hundred.

something to be said about a pit
open:    drawing you in    alive
can a pit close
          and still
      be a pit?

## A Song: Basic and Acidic

come right up, come right up
the money always sings
build your house on absence
devote yourself to things
build yourself an absence
money always sings

absence
tumescence
essence

tumescence precedes essence

absence recedes    receives tumescence

absence recedes    recedes    tumescence recedes

absence/tumesence

makes the heart

(seeds
another
story

I'll be with you, my father said, hair
as black as his eyes, I'll be with you
in two shakes of a dead lamb's tail

(I have never seen a lamb close-up
only cut-up on a plate)

Hit the tick, he said, and I thought
he meant to punch the clock, beat
its face in before the hands got
too high

his language
a tongue
not mine

All those hours listening to
'Jake and the Kid'  a little green light
steady on the radio  the language
brought home  not mine

and reading Mitchell—"the skeleton
requirements, simply," he says
"of land and sky"—I sense
the skeleton requires rock
and lake and bush (and sky)
(and fire?)

the prairies an overburden
prairie speech
an overburden

(I can hear my mother say  Horsefeathers
That's just horsefeathers and you know it)

## Sing While You Can

The orderly cleaned the razor, dipped and
honed and polished it.   He laid it shining
        big on the table
and laced my loins with foam.   He tugged
and stretched while I tried not to move/ not to
hear the snick snick of his deft strokes/ not to
        think   *my voice*
hoped he didn't want to make people orderly
        *rows and rows of neutral eyes neutral grey eyes*
knew why Nowlan hates the knacking wench
        *with razor and foam he*
bends low   swoops and snicks away
that badge of adult humanhood
        scratched and fingered
        for more than twenty years
leaves me a quivering target for the surgeon's knife
squeaky clean from stem to stern.
That foam has never been advertised on TV.

: The best way to clean off the sawdust is to hold the chunk under the corner of the truck and let the water wash it. Or you can throw it hard against the box when the driver is not looking and lick the broken side.

## 4.

something to be said about moving
earth    hauling dirt for fill
lug an old washtub
up and up the hill

: They loved to grow things so it wasn't a burden
to carry that dirt, build the soil and plant
a garden

one hill two hill
three hill down    mix in muskeg
damp and brown

: She helped too, it wasn't a burden—did a lot
of birthing as well, eight in all, seven survived,
each a blessing (in disguise).

stir in black dirt
clay and lime    mix in dry sand
take your time    turn it over in your mind

: Burden derives from the Anglo-Saxon *byrthen.*
Andrea was born at 2:25 PM Mountain Standard
time, November 22, 1983.
On that day Canada's population reached 25 million.
She's the one.

build a garden    mix in sand
haul the dirt there    all by hand

## The Solid Edge

If you live there long enough, you think of the world
as relative to north, relative to your edge of things.
This is what you know

: what a lake is (a gift of water)

: you sleep on bedrock (a bare skeleton)

When you want sky, you get rock and lake and
bush too, not overburden.
You get head frames
smoke stacks
smelter smoke (an over burden)

: the direction is clear (this is the point)

Your mind unfuzzed by a crazy grid of roads
coming at you and taking you off wildly in all
directions, you know what is where, and where is here.

: south is up hill    (*Take big steps*    my father says)

: water flowing to Hudson Bay is filtered by the silt
  of prairies, tickled by the roots of parkland trees

: money flows uphill    (a capital move)

: better not fish in Ross Lake    (a path in winter)

: home is easy to get to even if you know
  you can't live there

: the presence of an absence    (the lake is gone, the pit
                                              is there, an open cut)

: The scar moves thick down the right side of my belly dropping from rib cage to belt line. In the middle of my stomach, just lying there wishing only to be a scar, a round indentation where the belt buckle sits. Shannon says it looks like another belly button.    Just lying there.

## You Can Hear Him Mutter

### 1.

Standing on her out skirts *Kelsey Trail* perched firm on the rock a lumpy bumpkin statue designed by (blush) Al Capp. Don't believe it. FF cannot be seen. If you listen

: he says a glory hole
open cut
mine mine mine he says
The World's Only Baseball Diamond on
a Lake Bottom

He loved baseball and my mother too. She kept house at third base, swept everything clean, till a hard grounder kicked off a tuft of quack grass, skipped over a piece of slag and broke her nose.

Twice they moved kids and baggage—once from Creighton across the border to Flin Flon, and then another time they stretched up and added a second storey to the house. That summer a man fell off the roof and smashed his nose on a hammer. "He sure as hell wasn't going to let it go. Afraid it might get broken."

: he says tailings
slag pour

Down the basement there was: a furnace of many arms, a coal bin of mainly one colour, a sump with a big rock in the middle, a toilet collected weekly by the honey-men, their wagon parked on the hill in the lane. It may be your shit, but (you've heard) it's our bread and

2.

: he says    winter
boots
sliding
on fresh snow

bumshining

We pile into the Studebaker, tugging coats around ourselves, pinching legs and asses together, listening to hear if the motor will start. It catches, roars, the heater whines.

"All right, you guys stop breathing," he says. He scratches at the windshield, peeling thin slivers of snow just above the heater vents. The snow forms as fast as he scrapes it off.

He eases the car into gear, we move slowly    ka-thump    ka-thump    and he slumps down to peer through the half arc of clear windshield and    ka-thumpety    throws open his door to signal a left turn    ka-thumpety    we ka-thumpety down the hill, scrunching into collars, pinched asses, cold noses, crossed arms, fists    ka-thumpety    breathing    ka-thumpety

:        pass me the puck Bobby he says    pass me

We lived in the Rat Room when we weren't poking pool or playing hockey. It was a secret place: after the games and during public skating it was our room and we kept everyone else out. Two light bulbs, an open piss-trough with a wooden step in front, benches nailed to the wall, a few coat hooks, some bent nails, and thick black conveyor belt laid on the floor: we had it all to ourselves. Rink rats.

(So poor, he says pulling the toque down over his ears, we were so poor we didn't have hockey sticks. Used bent willow branches and horse apples for a puck and snot string for laces. We were so poor we ate turnips all the time.
At Christmas we got cranberry sauce with our turnips, and Mother cut off the bottoms of our pockets so we'd have something to play with.)

torn out    cut out

nowhere to be found

only the ending torn    out

nowhere to be found

3.

:     he says     grave
            yard
        shift
            boss
        sewer
            box

:   As the truck went by, Tom yelled, "Bumshiners!" The guy put his brakes on and slid about half a block down the street before he got stopped. By then we were across the sewer box and half way up the hundred steps.

running  along the CNR tracks
    boots squeaking on fresh snow
    past the creek bush to the bridge (next
    to the pond where in spring we collected tadpoles)
    we beat the train there    breaths puffing and chugging
    on the air    waiting    to see who could stand
    longest on the trestle before    jumping    as the train
    bore down steaming and we hoped the snow
    was soft below and not caked and
    the bridge (the train) trembled with
    the weight of the train    and the train train
    traintrain    traintrain    traintrain

## 4.

*Close the door*    he says  bending
down to give a bristle-bearded
whisker rub  *Were you born in a barn*?

(*Close that door*  he whispers)

—Flin Flon? Why the only people I've met from Flin Flon are hockey players and hookers.

—My mother is from Flin Flon!

—Oh.  And what position does she play?

Left wing, right wing, centre, defence, goal. The goal of life is something about a trace

of tongue tickling a lip

lipping a kiss and the rise

and fall of coming bliss

On a single weekend, my mother hit sixty-five, retired from her job and got married. They are not expecting children. (Her name is Burton now, but she's not a burden to me.)

To begin with, people build a roof overhead. Then they jack up the house, and put a basement under it. They need space between themselves, their beds, and bedrock. They know the earth moves.

Listen:

## TAILINGS

Quotations have been borrowed, and sometimes modified, from the following sources (other citations are situated in the text):

Valerie Hedman, Loretta Yauck, Joyce Henderson. *Flin Flon.* Flin Flon Historical Society, 1974.

Stephanie Jarvis, Lois Burke, Joyce Henderson. *Flin Flon: A Visual History, 1933-1983.* Flin Flon Jubilee Committee, 1983.

Jorge Luis Borges, with Margarite Guerrero. *The Book of Imaginary Beings.* Trans. Norman Thomas di Giovanni. New York: E.P. Dutton, 1978.

Irene Hewitt. "What's Yours Is Mine. Creighton vs Collins. Who Really Found Flin Flon?" *The Winnipeg Tribune Magazine* (May 24, 1980), pp. 8-10.

Charles Bramble. *The Land of the Lobstick: The Log of a Canoe Journey in The Pas District of Northern Manitoba.* Issued by J.A. Macdonald, Publicity Commissioner, Province of Manitoba, 1920.

A.G. Doughty and Chester Martin. *The Kelsey Papers.* Ottawa: The Public Archives of Canada and the Public Record Office of Northern Ireland, 1929.

J.E. Preston-Muddock. *The Sunless City.* London: F.V. White & Co., Ltd., 1905.

Douglas Durkin. *The Lobstick Trail: A Romance of Northern Canada.* Toronto: Musson, 1921.

Ruth and Jack Paterson. *Cranberry Portage: Frontier Life at the Crossroads of the North.* Vancouver: J.J. Douglas Ltd., 1974.

Lewis Mumford. *Technics and Civilization.* New York: Harcourt, World, & Brace, 1963.

*To the Arctic by Canoe, 1819-1821: The Journals and Paintings of Robert Hood, Midshipman with Franklin.* Ed. by C. Stuart Houston. McGill-Queen's University Press, 1974.

Alexander Henry. *Travels and Adventures in Canada and the Indian Territories Between the Years 1760 and 1776.* Ed. by James Bain. Rutland, Vermont: Charles E. Tuttle Co., 1969.